# JNDONESJA

## in pictures

VISUAL
GEOGRAPHY
SERIES

Prepared by **TOM GERST**

**STERLING PUBLISHING CO., INC.** NEW YORK

*Oak Tree Press Co., Ltd.*
Distributed by WARD LOCK, Ltd., London & Sydney

# VISUAL GEOGRAPHY SERIES

*The classic Indonesian features and shy smile of this young man can be found the length and breadth of the archipelago.*

Alaska
Argentina
Australia
Austria
Belgium and Luxembourg
Berlin—East and West
Brazil
Bulgaria
Canada
The Caribbean (English-
　Speaking Islands)
Ceylon
Chile
Colombia
Czechoslovakia
Denmark
Ecuador
England
Ethiopia
Finland
France
French Canada
Ghana
Greece
Guatemala
Hawaii
Holland
Honduras
Hong Kong
Hungary
Iceland
India
Indonesia
Iran
Iraq
Ireland
Israel

Italy
Jamaica
Japan
Kenya
Korea
Kuwait
Lebanon
Malaysia and Singapore
Mexico
Morocco
New Zealand
Norway
Pakistan
Panama and the Canal
　Zone
Peru
The Philippines
Poland
Portugal
Puerto Rico
Rumania
Russia
Scotland
South Africa
Spain
Sweden
Switzerland
Tahiti and the
　French Islands of
　the Pacific
Thailand
Turkey
Venezuela
Wales
West Germany
Yugoslavia

## PICTURE CREDITS

The publishers wish to thank the following for the photographs used in this book: Bell and Stanton, Inc.; Djambatan International Publishing House, Amsterdam; Indonesian Information Center, New York; Inter-Continental Hotels Corp.; Pan American World Airways; United Nations. The publishers also wish to thank Mr. Joop Ave, Consul of the Republic of Indonesia, New York, for his cooperation and assistance.

*C l*
*+*
*9/9./*
*S+*
*3/7/*

*A conical peak rises sharply above the rice fields. The terrain of Indonesia shows much evidence of volcanic action.*

# CONTENTS

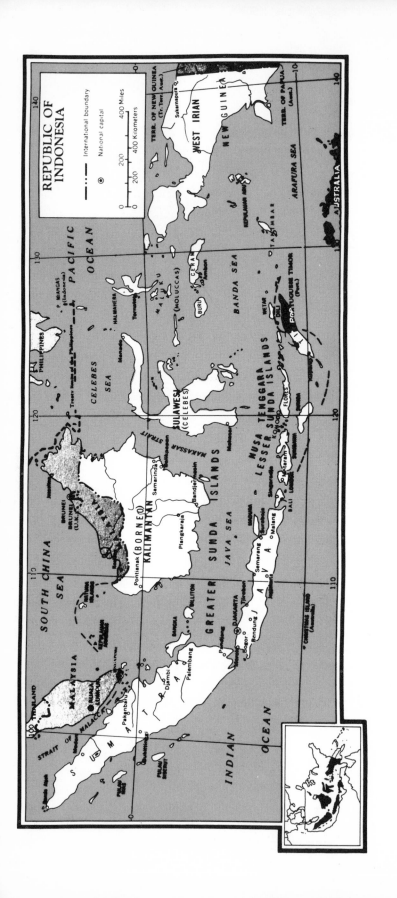

REPUBLIC OF
INDONESIA

International boundary
◉ National capital

0    200    400 Kilometers
0    200    400 Miles

*Driving along a serene country road in Java is a two-wheeled cart called a "sado" (from the French "dos-à-dos").*

# INTRODUCTION

PROBABLY NO NATION has had such diverse problems and long wait for independence as has Indonesia. A great chain of islands covering 3,000 miles between Asia and Australia, Indonesia is a blend of many peoples, cultures, religions, languages and philosophies. Though this very diversity has contributed to the problems of making one nation, it is also responsible, in part, for the fascination of the country to the student and traveller.

Indonesia might easily be compared to an eager and inquisitive child now come of age. For the country has, over the centuries, learned from every culture group which invaded its shores and adopted those things which it could use and which fitted the patterns of its own life.

Art forms, music and dance, religions, indeed all aspects of a culture were incorporated from the Malays, the Buddhists, the Arabs, the Chinese, the Hindus, and the Dutch, who at various times came to the islands.

Now, says Howard Palfrey Jones, a former United States ambassador to Indonesia, in an article in the Reader's Digest, "For the first time since it became a nation . . . Indonesia gives every evidence of having achieved both economic and political stability. With natural resources . . . that make it potentially the world's richest country after the United States and Russia, it appears embarked on a course which could put it first among the developing nations within a decade or two."

*A young man makes an offering of flowers to the sea goddess at Pelabuhan Ratu in West Java on the Indian Ocean. In the foreground is an image of the goddess, flanked by typical Indonesian puppets.*

*Like giant flights of steps, the terraced rice fields mount the hillsides of Bali.*

# I. THE LAND

THE REPUBLIC OF INDONESIA occupies most of the largest island group in the world—the Malay Archipelago, or East Indies, which also includes the Philippines and territories under the flags of Malaysia and Australia. It is made up of over 13,000 islands, of which some 6,000 are inhabited. The land area is 735,268 square miles, or about one-fifth the area of the United States, or six times as great as that of the British Isles.

Stretching over 3,000 miles in an arc from west of the Malay Peninsula south and east to West Irian (the western half of New Guinea), Indonesia lies between Southeast Asia and Australia. Indonesia has land boundaries with Malaysia, with which it shares the island of Borneo; with Portugal, which governs half of the island of Timor; and with Australia, which administers the eastern half of New Guinea. The island nation straddles the equator and

*The fabled island of Bali affords magnificent coastal views. The shrine, with its statue of a god, is to safeguard the fishermen who contribute so much to the island's food supply.*

separates the Indian and Pacific oceans, including within its far-flung reaches many seas, notably the Java Sea, the Flores Sea and the Banda Sea.

The islands of Indonesia are generally divided into four main groups:

The Greater Sunda Islands include Java and Madura, Sulawesi (Celebes), Sumatra and Kalimantan (Borneo minus East Malaysia).

The Lesser Sunda Islands, or Nusa Tenggara, comprise Lombok and Bali, Sumbawa, Flores, Sumba, Alor, Komodo, Savu, Roti, Wetar and Timor.

The Maluku (Molucca) Islands are Halmahera, Ternate, Tidore, Moti, Makian, Morotai, Batjan, Obi, Ceram, Buru, Ambon (Amboina), Banda, Babar, and the Aru, Tanimbar and Kai groups.

West Irian (the western half of New Guinea) and the surrounding islands of Waigeo, Biak, Misool and Japen form the fourth group.

Sumatra, the largest island wholly within Indonesia, and sixth largest in the world, is

182,000 square miles in area, roughly the size of West Virginia and California combined, or somewhat larger than Sweden. It is also the most volcanic region in the archipelago. Java, most important of the islands, is the home of

*"Buffalo Canyon," in the Padang Highlands near Bukit Tinggi on Sumatra, affords one of the most impressive views in all of Indonesia.*

*Periangan Mountain, called locally "Papandajan," is located in the western part of Java, not far from Bandung. The picture was taken from Tjisurupan, a tourist resort near the town of Garut.*

two-thirds of Indonesia's population, yet comprises only one-seventh of the country's total land mass. The majority of Indonesia's rice is grown on this island, which is also one of the main sources of petroleum and tea.

## TOPOGRAPHY

A simple division of the country's land mass would be lowlands, high plains and mountainous areas. The lowlands are found along the coasts of the major islands and river valleys. The high plains are often dried-up mountain lakes or flat stretches connecting the mountainous areas. The mountains and volcanoes are of major interest.

Indonesia is a largely mountainous country with a central range extending the length of the archipelago. The highest mountain, Mt. Sukarno in West Irian, rises 15,300 feet. Over 400 volcanoes are located throughout the country, 100 of which are active. Bali's main volcano, Gunung Agung, sacred as the home of the gods, erupted last in 1963 killing some 1,600 people. The most spectacular volcano in recent history is Krakatoa, or Krakatau, a small volcanic island in the Sunda Strait between Java and Sumatra. In 1883 the island volcano erupted with such force that some of its debris landed in Madagascar on the other side of the Indian Ocean.

Geologists tend to believe that in prehistoric times the western islands were part of the Asian continent and the eastern ones part of Australia. It is thought that, during the earth's long

**9**

*Bamboo poles are tied together and floated down river to the mills and markets in the cities.*

period of formation, the water rose and submerged all but the higher portions of the mountain range, forming the Indonesian archipelago. It is even possible that Sumatra and the Asian mainland were connected as late as the time of Christ.

## RIVERS

Though Indonesia has many rivers, none is comparable in size to those in Europe, Asia or Africa. For example, the Musi River on Sumatra is navigable by ocean-going vessels of 10,000 tons for only 80 miles. Indonesia's rivers do provide, in varying degrees, a means of transportation on most of the islands and on

*Beautiful views abound in Indonesia, as evidenced by this scene of a charming brook on the east coast of Sumatra, near the town of Belawan.*

*As in other parts of Asia, many people live in river boats. This is a view of Palembang on the Musi River in Sumatra.*

some they are the only means of communication and transportation. They have a great potential for generating electrical power and are playing an important part in the country's development schemes. So far, river development has been concentrated on Java, where comparatively small rivers have supplied most of the electricity. The government's plans place great emphasis on the production of electrical power.

## CLIMATE

The tropical climate of Indonesia is attributable to its torrid zone location, straddling the equator. Though temperatures normally range between 66 and 96 degrees, the average temperature at sea level is 79 degrees. Mountain and ocean breezes effect a one-degree cooling of temperature for every 300 feet of elevation above sea level.

Weather in the archipelago is determined by the monsoons, winds that bring either dry or wet weather, depending on the season. Although rainfall is abundant the year round, "wet seasons" are brought in with the west monsoon from the Indian Ocean, and generally last from November to March. "Dry seasons" are ushered in after an interim period of about two months, with the east monsoon coming from the dry interior of Australia, usually between June and October. Humidity is always high and

*An impressive milestone in Indonesia's march of progress is the Djatiluhur Dam in West Java here seen under construction.*

*The tall, spindly kapok, or silk-cotton, tree yields a fibrous material, also called kapok, which is a major export of the country.*

## FLORA AND FAUNA

### PLANTS

Indonesia's rich soil and tropical climate have given rise to a wide variety of vegetation. The rafflesia, for example, is one of the world's most curious plants. It grows upon shrubs and vines, sending fibrous roots into them, and when it produces its single, giant flower, only the flower is visible, all other external parts having withered away. Rafflesia flower blooms measuring 36 inches across and bamboo stalks 3 inches thick are not uncommon. One of the best known flowers is the beautiful frangipani, chiefly grown in Bali, where it is widely used for temple decorations.

Most of the fruit consumed in Indonesia is cultivated, including the banana, breadfruit, citrus fruits, guava, mango, papaya, pineapple and tamarind. But a large number of edible fruits grow wild, most of them unknown in the West.

Indonesia's forests contain many kinds of trees such as camphor, sandalwood, oak, chestnut, rhododendron, fig, banyan, and, in the high mountain forests, conifers. The most commercially important trees in the islands are the coconut, rubber and bamboo.

Nearly two-thirds of Indonesia's land area is covered with dense forests. In the coastal areas, these forests are largely mangrove and nipa palm, while tropical rain forests predominate in the interior lowlands. In Java and Madura, management is devoted mainly to the teak forests and several other species whose timber is valuable. When additional roads are built in the tropical rain forests on Java a greatly increased wood supply will be available for domestic use and for export.

Indonesia's forests are classified either as National Forests or Community Forests. The National Forests are further divided into teak and non-teak forests by government regulation. The Community Forests are formally included in the National Forests, but actually are treated as community property by the people of the district.

The rain forests of Sumatra and Kalimantan are characterized by their lush and ever green

the heaviest rains fall in the mountains, averaging 240 inches annually in some regions. Average annual rainfall in Djakarta is 80 inches and 120 to 144 inches in Sumatra and Kalimantan. Some small islands, such as Komodo, are extremely dry, covered with grass and sparsely provided with trees, but they are exceptional.

Indonesian days and nights are much the same length, with only a 48-minute difference between the longest and the shortest day. Twilights are extremely short in duration—the sun seems to plunge into the horizon—with night almost directly following the daylight.

For the traveller to Indonesia, November and April are considered the least pleasant months. Most tourists arrive during the west monsoon, mainly because it corresponds with the winter months of the northern part of the world. However, no month is really unsuited for travel.

*Workers pose beside a giant banyan tree, giving an idea of the great size these trees attain. A kind of fig, the banyan sends roots down from its branches, which in time become secondary trunks. An old tree may have dozens of trunks and cover a large area.*

appearance. Tidal forests, which are kept lush by flooding, can also be found on the two islands, and are important sources of charcoal, fuel wood, small timber and tannin.

Realizing the importance of its forests, Indonesia created the Directorate General of Forestry, under the Department of Agriculture to carry out the organization of forestry.

*Past a rice paddy, a boy rides one water buffalo, while leading another by a rope.*

Management of the forests is handled by the Forest Service and State Forest Enterprise, in coordination with the Directorate General. Additional projects of importance include reforestation and the management of wildlife and the national parks. The latter two are of special interest to national and international tourism.

Production of timber in the teak forests is carried out mainly by men with the aid of work animals. Attempts at mechanization have proved difficult, due to a lack of skilled manpower. The need for a vast worker force in the forests has been drawing employees from overpopulated areas where jobs were scarce. The State Forest Enterprise supervises the harvesting and marketing of teak. Private contractors handle the majority of non-teak timber production.

Other forest products are seeds used for drugs and dyes, rattan, resin, and cajuput oil (used in treating skin diseases). These are gathered by local people and marketed by private enterprise or by the State Forest Enterprise.

*Found in many areas of Indonesia, the mouse-deer, or chevrotain, is not a true deer. The smallest of all ruminants (hoofed, cud-chewing mammals), it measures only 10 to 14 inches high at the shoulder.*

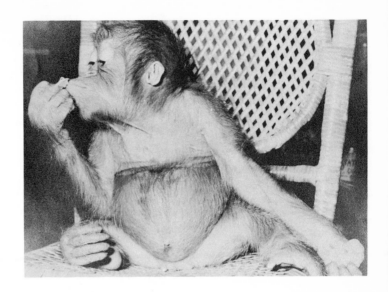

*A young orang-utan enjoys a snack. Peculiar to Sumatra and Java, the orang-utan is one of the great apes, an Oriental counterpart of Africa's gorillas and chimpanzees.*

## ANIMALS

Animal life tends to be Asian in character in the western and central parts of the archipelago, and Australian in the eastern. In Sumatra, Java and Bali, panthers and tigers can be found. Elephants, now extinct in Java, inhabit Sumatra and Kalimantan.

Rhinoceroses can also be seen on two of the islands—the one-horned rhino on Java and the twin-horned on Sumatra. Orang-utans and gibbons are found in Sumatra and parts of Java, while the small grey monkey abounds as far east as Bali. The wily *kantjil* (chevrotain) plays a rôle in Indonesian fairy tales similar to the fox in western folklore. The water baffalo is domesticated in Indonesia and is the farmer's primary work animal. Wild boar, deer, crocodiles and lizards are common.

The island of Komodo is famous for its monitor, the world's largest lizard, called *ora* by the Indonesians. This creature, which may attain a length of 10 feet, stalks its prey through the dry grasslands of its home.

The Maluku islands are renowned for their great variety of beautiful parrots, and West Irian is famous for its birds of paradise. Other birds to be found in Indonesia include cockatoos, ducks, kingfishers, pheasants, pigeons and peacocks. Snakes include the huge python, which coils its thick body round its prey, crushing it to death, then swallowing the entire animal. Marine life is abundantly represented by many kinds of fish, mollusks, crustaceans, sharks and octopuses.

*The world's only living prehistoric lizards, the Komodo monitors, are found only on 4 small islands including Komodo, for which the lizards were named. They may reach 10 feet in length!*

**15**

*The tin on the islands of Banka and Billiton off the coast of Sumatra is one of Indonesia's many natural resources. The mining method seen here is suction-dredging of the tin contained in sand and clay banks. Tin-bearing clay banks are flooded, causing them to crumble into the water. The resulting mud is pumped into machines which spray it out, causing the ore to separate from the clay.*

## NATURAL RESOURCES

The mineral wealth of Indonesia is vast and, for the better part, unexploited. Tin and petroleum are of major importance. Deposits of bauxite, iron ore, coal, asphalt, manganese, copper, nickel, wolframite, sulphur, iodine, gold, silver, platinum and diamonds are yet to be fully developed.

Teak, ebony, sandalwood and ironwood are products of the country's forests. There are also plentiful stands of bamboo and rattan, mangrove bark for tanning and, important to the manufacture of varnish and lacquer, indigo and copal.

## CITIES

### DJAKARTA

The city of Djakarta, built on the site of the ancient port town of Sunda Kelapa, is the capital of the country, and approximately 4,500,000 people live and work there. The city has had several names — first, Sunda Kelapa, then Djajakarta, then Batavia (a name be-

stowed on it by the Dutch), and, when independence came, the present one, a shortened version of Djajakarta.

It is a bustling city, crowded and picturesque, where traffic is a problem, as in any large city. Architecturally it is a mixture of styles and improvizations upon Oriental and Western designs. Some of the old Dutch houses date from the 17th century.

There are department stores, market places and open-air shops, ancient hotels and modern ones, vendors who ply their wares house-to-house and along the main streets. Notable, too, is a museum which has a fine collection of Oriental porcelain.

Tandjung Priok is the port for Djakarta and offers seaside recreation areas, as well.

### BOGOR

The residential town of Bogor, 33 miles from Djakarta, is known for its botanical garden,

*Midday traffic jams in the business district of Djakarta can be as great as in any Western metropolis.*

*The new Cultural Centre in Djakarta, is one of the showplaces of the country's capital city.*

which covers some 275 acres. The original official residence of the Dutch Governors is situated there, and is now used by the President of the Republic. North of the city is the Puntjak Mountain region, which is a holiday area for the citizens of Djakarta. The district has many hotels, swimming pools, gardens and golf courses, in a setting of great natural beauty.

### BANDUNG

Bandung, the capital of the Province of West Java, is located southeast of Djakarta on a plateau some 2,000 feet high and has a population of nearly 1,000,000. The city was founded by the Dutch in 1810, as a military headquarters, and grew quickly into a major industrial and scientific hub. North of the city is the holiday resort of Lembang. Bandung played host to the historic Asian-African Conference in 1955.

### JOGJAKARTA AND SURAKARTA

Jogja and Solo are the popular names for Jogjakarta and Surakarta. Approximately 40 miles apart and 310 miles from Djakarta, these two cities of Java have long histories and both have been cultural capitals. Jogja has a population of 900,000 and Solo, 400,000. They have many historically famous buildings and temples within their immediate area and near by. Gadjah Mada University is located in Jogja, while Solo was for centuries the home of the Sultans of Solo, whose great walled palace remains.

*A young merchant of Bogor rests on his way to market with his heavy load of pottery.*

*Deer are an important part of the wild life of Indonesia. These were photographed in the park of the Presidential summer palace in Bogor.*

## MEDAN

Medan is a fairly new city, having been a village only some 80 years ago. It is now the largest city on Sumatra and is the capital of the Province of North Sumatra, with a population of over 500,000. Indonesia's largest mosque is here, as is the palace of the Sultan of Deli.

## DEN PASAR

Den Pasar is really more of a small town than a city, although it is the largest on the island of Bali. However, its growth is expected to be rapid within the near future, now that an

*Rubber tires on an oxcart provide a contrast between old and new, in this scene near Jogjakarta.*

*On the island of Sumatra, these Minangkabau houses in the Padang Highlands look like the hulls of great ships resting on pilings.*

international airport has been completed on its outskirts.

### PADANG AND BUKIT TINGGI

Padang, the capital city of Central Sumatra, is on the west coast of the island. Flying time from Djakarta is three hours. Bukit Tinggi, 57 miles from Padang, is a more important city and is located in one of the most beautiful parts of the country. A notable attraction in Bukit Tinggi is the museum in the zoological garden.

*A quiet residential street on the outskirts of Djakarta is lined with some of the newer and more solidly built houses currently being erected.*

**19**

*Borobudur is one of the most famous monuments in Indonesia, located just north of the city of Jogja-karta. Not a temple in the sense of a building in which people can congregate for worship, but rather a kind of monumental shrine, Borobudur was probably erected in the 8th century and is a creation of Hindu Javanese art.*

# 2. HISTORY

THE ORIGINS OF THE early inhabitants of the Indonesian archipelago are cloaked in antiquity. In 1890, Dr. Eugene Dubois discovered the fossilized remains of the now famous "Java Man," validating man's habitation of this island during an early stage of his evolution. Subsequent archeological finds indicate that an even earlier form of man made his home on the archipelago over 500,000 years ago.

It is believed that the first true men in Indonesia included several different dark-skinned peoples, some Negroid, and others resembling the aborigines of Australia and the Papuans of New Guinea.

## THE MALAYS

About 3000 B.C., during the Neolithic Age, it is thought that the short, stocky, brown-skinned Malay people settled in the archipelago as far east as the western Moluccas, beginning a series of migratory movements from the mainland. This invasion brought with it stone implements, techniques for constructing wooden houses, weaving, pottery-making, and the cultivation of rice.

At the same time, the Malay Peninsula itself was being overrun by light-skinned Mongols from the north who, through assimilation,

*One of the many statues of Buddha on the terraces of Borobudur, this one shows the lotus position. Other statues are enclosed in the round bell-shaped structures to the left and behind.*

altered the physical characteristics of the Malay people. When the second great migration of Malays was made to the Indonesian archipelago during the Bronze Age, the newcomers were decidedly Mongoloid. They spread as far east as New Guinea. Settling along the coasts they forced their predecessors into the inland areas. To this day, Mongol physical characteristics are more prevalent along the coasts.

A later influx of peoples from the north brought an even more highly developed culture which was absorbed by the "Indonesians" already in existence.

## HINDUS AND ARABS

Invasion from Hindu India further influenced not only the physical characteristics of the people but their religion and language as well. The Hindus first came as missionaries and traders, but gradually gained control of large areas, and a number of great Hindu and Buddhist empires arose. The Arabs followed the Hindus and have exercised perhaps the greatest influence of all. About 90 per cent of the Indonesian people are Moslems today, as a result of Arab infiltration. By 1600, Islam had replaced Hinduism and Buddhism as the chief religion. However, under Islam the country broke up into many small states, or sultanates.

## EUROPEANS

The first European known to have visited Indonesia was Marco Polo who, in 1292, journeyed to Java and northern Sumatra. A little more than two centuries later, in 1511, the roots of Western dominance were planted with the Portuguese landing at Malacca on the Malay Peninsula, "in search of Christians and spices." (One of the driving forces of the Portuguese was the search for a legendary lost Christian kingdom in Asia.) The Spanish, Dutch, French and English soon followed and carried on a colonial struggle for the prize of Indonesia's vast wealth.

In 1565, the Portuguese were defeated and expelled from the archipelago, except for eastern Timor, by the combined military action of the Indonesian sultanates. Spain withdrew from most of the archipelago after the defeat of its Armada by the English in 1588, retaining the Philippine Islands. French colonial ambitions were never realized beyond a few campaigns in a very small part of Java.

## DUTCH RULE

By the end of the 16th century, only the Dutch and English were left to contest the immensely profitable trade of the Indies. During the middle of the 17th century, England's world-wide commitments drained its ability to meet the Dutch concentration of effort in Indonesia and the British withdrew from the struggle. The Netherlands East India Company, founded in 1602, was then free to establish a complete Indonesian monopoly by

*The famous Hindu temple of Prambanan, where the equally famous Ramayama Ballet is now performed. At night, the ancient monuments are flood-lighted making an impressive background for the performance.*

1623. Although the company prospered for a time, the Netherlands government revoked its charter in 1790, because of mismanagement and corruption and the government itself assumed full administration of the islands 10 years later.

Indonesia, in its natural state, was a veritable pot of gold to the Western colonists. Spices, indigo, gems and dozens of other items valued in Europe and America represented untold wealth. The island nation's economy became highly organized to serve Western needs.

In the 19th century, new systems to harvest this wealth were imposed, notably in agriculture. Farmers were forced to grow produce which would bring good prices in new world-wide markets. The Indonesian farmer was unprepared emotionally or technically for this change, and resentment and unrest became great and deep-seated.

*Of the many colonial wars fought by the Dutch in Indonesia, the North Sumatra War of 1873–1903 was one of the longest. Here a Dutch general and his staff observe the attack on Batee Ilie in 1901.*

In addition to being a supplier for the Dutch traders, the country and its people were forced to become a market for Western goods which needed a large and ready outlet. Cotton products, for example, were brought in, replacing native materials. This caused further and extensive disruption to the domestic culture.

The repressive system of state-controlled exploitation to extract revenue for the Netherlands was enforced until 1877. In that year liberal Dutch demands on their government led to the abandonment of this harsh system and its replacement by private exploitation.

The archipelago's history prior to and fol-

*Sukarno (third from left) and co-defendants are on trial at Bandung in 1930, for revolutionary activity.*

*During the War of Independence in the 1940's, Indonesian guerrillas man a jungle outpost near Djakarta.*

lowing this change in colonial policy was marked by numerous rebellions and local wars. The more notable of these were: the revolt in the Moluccas (1831–1837); the Java War (1825–1830); the Padri War in West Sumatra (1830–1836); the Atjeh War in North Sumatra (1873–1903); the wars in Palembang (South Sumatra), Goa (South Celebes), South Kalimantan and Bali from 1903–1908.

## THE RISE OF NATIONALISM

On May 20, 1908, an association called the Budi-Utomo (Sublime Effort) was founded by a group of medical students and intellectuals in Batavia (Djakarta). Originally formed as a cultural association, it soon turned to political opposition to colonial oppression. Because this group has been acknowledged as the forerunner of the Indonesian nationalist government, May 20th is celebrated each year as "National Awakening Day."

Many independence movements followed during the next three decades. The two more important factions to come into being were the Indonesian Communist Party (PKI), established in May, 1920, and the Indonesian Nationalist Party, formed in July, 1927, by Sukarno and other leaders. (Sukarno, who later became the leader of his country's liberation movement, had no other name than Sukarno.)

## WORLD WAR II

The Japanese occupation of the archipelago (March 9, 1942 to August 14, 1945) aided the nationalist cause. With Japan's defeat, Sukarno and Hatta proclaimed the Indonesian Republic on August 17, 1945. Their Declaration of Independence, called "Pantja-Sila," was based on the five principles of belief—One Supreme God, Civilized Humanity, Nationalism, Democracy and Social Justice. It expresses the country's basic philosophy upon which the government was built and upon which it operates. The Indonesian Constitution adopted on August 18, 1945, allowed for strong Presidential powers, a Parliament, a Supreme Advisory Council, a State Finance Comptrolling Body and a People's Consultative Assembly (Madjelis Permusjawarstan Rakjat). The red and white national flag was accepted as well as a national common language, Bahasa Indonesia. Sukarno was elected President and Mohammad Hatta, Vice-President.

On September 5, 1945, a Presidential Cabinet was formed with President Sukarno as Premier. The new state was divided into the eight provinces of Sumatra, Kalimantan, Sulawesi, Tae Moluccas, the Lesser Sundas and West, Central and East Java. Djakarta (formerly Batavia) was designated as the national capital.

In December, 1947, the Dutch transferred sovereignty to the Indonesians. At the formal ceremony in the Royal Palace in Amsterdam are the late Queen Wilhelmina of the Netherlands (middle) and, at her right, Mohammad Hatta.

## THE WAR OF INDEPENDENCE

The Dutch, however, did not accept the legality of the newly established Indonesian Republic or its provisional government. In an attempt to re-establish its control over the islands, the Netherlands sent armed forces. Bitter hostilities and occasional negotiations ended finally when the United Nations interceded and a cease-fire was effected in August, 1949. The Round Table Conference held at The Hague between representatives of the Netherlands and Indonesia concluded with the transfer of sovereignty from the Netherlands to a newly-created Republic of the United States of Indonesia on December 27, 1949.

The Republic was a loose federation of 16 states, each with its own executive branch, cabinet and legislative body. Additionally, each state sent representatives to the federal legislative body in Djakarta. Sukarno and Mohammad Hatta were again selected for the Presidency and Vice-Presidency. Within a year, on August 17, 1950, all member states voted to dissolve their individual governments and merge into the single Republic of Indonesia. The Federal Government was dissolved and a new centralized state and constitution were adopted.

## COMMUNISM

As happens with many under-developed and emerging nations, Communism gains great and strong holds upon the masses. Such was the case in Indonesia. The Communist Party, PKI, was one of the oldest political movements in Indonesia, with roots in the Dutch Colonial period. Marching under a flag of liberation from oppression, hunger, social injustices and the like, it won an army of adherents.

Following World War II, the party gained power and members. The country, torn by the Japanese occupation, was hungry, since the rice supply, the main sustainer of life, had been exported to Japan. With a new untried government in power, Communism daily played a more important rôle in Indonesian political life, especially as President Sukarno adopted a stand of increasing withdrawal from co-operation with the West and hostility toward Malaysia. The movement's influence was growing more noticeable locally and internationally. So much so, that many world observers considered Indonesia lost to the international brotherhood of democratic nations.

On the night of September 30, 1965, an incident occurred which was to alter drastically and completely the current history of the country. Gangs of young Communists captured and murdered six leading generals who held high positions in the government.

This violent act touched off a reign of terror during the ensuing months. Loyal Indonesians rose up across the archipelago and eliminated thousands of Communists. The number is merely an educated guess on the part of some witnesses. The real number is unknown, perhaps unknowable.

**25**

*President Suharto and his family pose for an official portrait.*

In retrospect, however, figures are unimportant. What is important is that a change in Indonesian politics and government was made possible. "In those first days of October, following the coup, it was touch and go," said a Western observer. "The army moved decisively but it didn't know it would win." But it won, and order was eventually restored.

In July, 1966, a new Cabinet was formed and came into office. It was restructured in 1967 with "the principal aim of bringing about simplification and of improving the working efficiency necessary for the pure implementation of the 1945 Constitution," in the words of a government publication.

Acting President was General Suharto with Sri Sultan Hamengku Buwono IX as Minister of State, and Adam Malik as Minister of Foreign Affairs. General Suharto was subsequently raised to President, replacing President Sukarno who was put into involuntary retirement, in which state he died in 1970. Sukarno remained a national hero and was buried with all the dignity of his rank.

As for Communism, President Suharto said in his speech at the end of 1969, "The New Order does not merely ban the Communist Party PKI and prevent the comeback of the PKI and the Old Order, but has in the first place to transform the mental attitude, pattern of thinking and methods of working of us all."

*General Suharto, President of the Republic of Indonesia, addresses the Assembly in the modern Parliament Building. Women, it is obvious, play an important rôle in the country's government.*

# 3. THE GOVERNMENT

INDONESIA'S POLITICAL structure has changed several times since independence was won. The provisional constitution of 1950, modelled after Western parliamentary systems, provided for a President with limited power, a unicameral (one-house) legislature and a cabinet responsible to the legislature. The present constitution calls for a different distribution of power, with the President playing a much more dominant rôle.

## EXECUTIVE

The President, the highest executive of the Government, holds office for a 5-year term and is eligible for re-election. In administering the State, authority and responsibility are in the hands of the President. The Ministers of State, who are his assistants and are responsible to him only, are concerned with special aspects of economic and social activity, as well as with

*Two young sailors gaze across the water as cruisers of the Indonesian navy stand by.*

government administration—e.g. one Minister of State heads an Office for the Improvement of State Apparatus.

In addition to the Ministers of State, there are the regular Cabinet Ministers, appointed by the President, and responsible for defence, foreign affairs, justice, information, finance, manpower and the other areas of national activity which are customarily controlled by a Cabinet Ministry.

## LEGISLATURE

The Parliament, known as the Dewan Perwakilan Rajat, shares legislative power with the President. The 253 members of Parliament are appointed by the President and are drawn from political parties, trade unions, farmers groups, and regional organizations throughout the 19 Indonesian provinces.

The Parliament also functions as part of a much larger People's Consultative Assembly. This Assembly is comprised of some 800 members and incorporates, in addition to the Parliament, a People's Council of Representatives and other delegates. It is distinguished from the legislative body proper and sits at least once in every 5-year period, but it may be called into session in times of emergency. Its primary purpose is to apply the Constitution

in determining broad lines of policy for the government. It elects the President and Vice-President, and its members are chosen in the national election.

## OTHER BRANCHES

Indonesia's leaders also have access to the advice of two special agencies. These are the Supreme Advisory Council, which is composed of representatives of political parties and special-interest groups, and the National Planning Council, which is made up of delegates from regional and other groups.

The highest judicial body is the Supreme Court, or Mahkamah Agung.

## THE INDONESIAN COAT-OF-ARMS

The National Coat-of-Arms of the Republic of Indonesia symbolizes the Indonesian people and country, their history and characteristics.

The golden-hued garuda (a mythical, eagle-like bird), the dominant figure in the design, represents the awakened strength of Indonesia and its "Golden Victory." The chain and shield suspended from the garuda's neck are symbolic of the struggle to achieve and defend Indonesia's freedom.

*General Suharto was named President by the Consultative Assembly on March 27, 1968.*

## FAMILY PLANNING

In the field of family planning, activity was noticeably increased in 1969. Approximately 300 family planning clinics now exist, many of which are extensions of family welfare offices previously established. General information is disseminated and data collected to assist in future development. As with most Asian countries, population growth is a real problem, not only for immediately housing and feeding, but in the future for educating and finding employment for citizens.

## TRANSMIGRATION

Transmigration, meaning the relocation of Indonesian citizens, is necessary for many areas and is a gigantic government undertaking.

Java, the most heavily populated of the islands can no longer support all of its inhabitants, whereas Sumatra and other areas need additional people to work the land.

For economic and humane reasons the transmigration scheme is important. The government, wishing to make the moves attractive to the people and as painless as possible, offers transportation, land, a house, and food sufficient until the first harvest to those families who agree to relocate.

In 1969, some 6,000 migrants left Java and Bali to live in South Sumatra, the Risu Islands

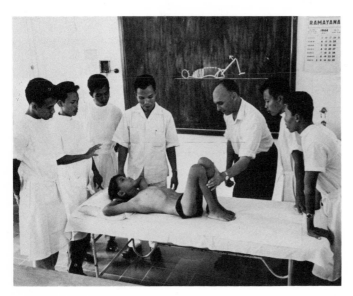

*The Indonesian Government is making great efforts to raise health standards. Here a World Health Organization expert gives a demonstration to trainees at the Rehabilitation Centre in Solo, central Java.*

and South Sulawesi. Rice fields, as well as other farm projects, are being started where none existed before.

An additionally important aspect of transmigration will be the increased productivity of the land, and easing of the unemployment situation, producing a rise in the gross national product.

## WEST IRIAN

West Irian (formerly Netherlands New Guinea) was a major source of disagreement between Indonesia and the Netherlands for 13 years after independence was gained. The Netherlands continued to administer the area, while Indonesia believed it should be a part of the Republic. The matter was settled in 1962, with the signing of the New York Agreement at the United Nations headquarters.

The agreement provided that the United Nations' Temporary Executive Authority would take over the West Irian administration in October and hand it over to Indonesia on May 1, 1963, provided the people of West Irian wished to join the Republic. This was to be determined by vote, according to the agreement and called an Act of Free Choice.

Indonesia was successful in the vote over the Netherlands. It is now the task of the Republic to improve the primitive conditions of the area and develop its agriculture and natural resources. Technicians are being sent to West Irian and an educational plan has been started. Funds for these projects are being raised within the Republic and abroad.

*Very different from the standard Indonesian type are these villagers in West Irian. Note the variety of dress—and undress— from modern to tribal.*

*Rice fields surround a typical village located along one of the roads of Bali. Each village has its own temple and is self-governing. All citizens contribute time and work to such village projects as road repairs.*

# 4. THE PEOPLE

APPROXIMATELY 80 per cent of 113,000,000 Indonesians live in villages scattered across the huge archipelago. It is estimated that there are some 44,000 villages! The dominant Malay type is most common in the western islands, while the dark-skinned races appear most often in the east. In addition, there are some people of partly Dutch descent, and a sizable Chinese population in some cities.

By and large, the village is a closely knit social unit which handles its own local affairs.

In Bali, for instance, each person is expected to contribute time and effort on village projects such as road building and improvement, building schools, or caring for the temple.

As part of the 5-year development plan, each village was allotted certain monies by the central government in 1969 for improvements. Not only was this necessary for nationwide progress, but it also has helped increase and strengthen ties between the people and the government in Djakarta. The money is used

*In a communal dwelling, such as this one on the edge of the jungle, several related families live together and share common work, religious and leisure projects.*

for the construction of markets, bridges, irrigation systems, schools and other group requirements. The plan has given the people a sense of involvement in their own development and destinies.

Additionally, emphasis is to be placed on health, and Public Health Offices will be established in each village, These facilities, among other things, will help expand sanitation and immunization projects.

Backing up the government's health plan is rehabilitation of existing hospitals and completion of a number of regional hospitals. With the completion of new hospitals, the country now has a total of 941, making available some 82,548 beds.

## LANGUAGE

Indonesian, Malay, Javanese and other related tongues belong to a far-flung language family, the Malayo-Polynesian, which also includes the languages of the Philippines and of most of the South Pacific Islands.

A high cultural level has existed in Indonesia for centuries. The first written samples of the Malay language, for example, are stone inscriptions dating from A.D. 680. The language used was developed to such a point that it might well qualify as literature. Additionally, Chinese records of the 6th century refer to a language called Kwun Lun used for teaching religious sciences. Astronomy and mathematics were known. It is thought that Kwun Lun was probably the Malay language or a Malay dialect.

Another early language was Javanese, though there is no existing written proof of this. Still, considering the magnificent temples and buildings in central Java dating from the 8th century and earlier, it follows that such a highly developed culture must have had a highly developed language.

Recorded literary creations date from the 15th century, in a language referred to as Old Malay or Classic Malay. By the time the Portuguese and Dutch arrived in Indonesia, Malay was the commercial language used throughout most of the islands. From then on, the language absorbed many elements from a variety of sources—Dutch, Portuguese, and Arabic—resulting in today's national language called "Bahasa Indonesia," derived from Malay. It has been generally accepted and is taught in schools and used throughout the islands. Many dialects, however, persist, and are used locally. English is taught as the second language. Indonesian is written in the Latin alphabet.

*Indonesia's educational efforts include extensive adult projects, as well as the usual ones for children and young people.*

## EDUCATION

It is amazing that in an area which has had a highly developed and complex culture, education has only recently become widespread.

The Dutch, who administered the islands for three and a half centuries, did not promote education. Whether this was just laxness, lack of consideration and thought, or a deliberate omission in order to make control easier, is debatable. But the fact remains that schools were few and illiteracy high.

In 1941, at the outbreak of the war in the Pacific, Indonesia had no qualified univeristy. Even Java, the most highly developed area socially, economically and educationally, had only a few colleges. Students who had wanted, and could afford, higher education had to go to

*Students of the Islamic Teachers' Academy pore over their books. Note the modern school bag (lower left) in contrast to the traditional dress.*

*The modern buildings of the University for Engineering at Bandung have been designed to utilize the Batak-styled roofs typical of local architecture.*

Europe, mainly Holland, to study. The cost to all but a few was prohibitive.

It is little wonder, in the light of the educational deficiencies, that Indonesia was so long in awakening and gaining independence.

The Dutch rule was based on an "ethical" policy. This meant keeping local customs and administering through them. Modern ideas and principles were considered dangerous. It was not until 1908, when the group of medical students in Djakarta founded the association named the "Budi Utomo" (Sublime Effort), that the beginnings of change occurred.

At the time of independence in 1945 the literacy rate was put at only 7 per cent of the total population. One of the first actions the new government took was an improved education scheme. Within 5 years the number of schools increased from a mere 3,000 to over 35,000 and the number of pupils from under

*Young women of eastern Indonesia are now learning to operate sewing machines.*

*Children on their way to school are the same the world over. These smiling faces were photographed in Djakarta.*

*At the Indonesian Technical College, a leading school for the study of Asian arts, students are trained in traditional and contemporary styles.*

2,000,000 to over 5,000,000. Universities and colleges were also developed and the great effort continues with increasingly good results.

As of 1969, approximately 17 per cent of the national budget was devoted to education in one form or another.

This vast undertaking includes not only the young people of the country but the middle and older age groups as well. Adult education courses are popular and are increasing.

Included in the educational scheme are the Manpower Training Projects. These were begun in 1969 at Pasar Rebo (Djakarta), Bandung, Singasari, Semarang, Jogjakarta and elsewhere. Education is an important aspect of President General Suharto's government's 5-year plan. To increase the gross national product, improve the economy, and develop generally, education, training and skills are required.

A significant, though not overwhelmingly large, contribution has been made in the area of education training by foreign companies which operate in Indonesia. Training courses have been set up for the local employees by many of the industrial and service companies. The result has been a substantial growth in the skilled worker market.

Training and educational assistance have come to the country from many nations and world organizations. Technical teams have worked and are still working in the country. However, considering the vastness of Indonesia and the years of neglect and no effort, it will be some time before a general education will be widely available.

## RELIGIOUS INFLUENCES

During the first century A.D., Hindu traders arrived from India and soon were followed by Buddhist immigrants who spread their highly developed, sophisticated culture and religion

At Jogjakarta's Leather Research Institute, third-year trainees await the results of a classroom experiment. Leather and leather products play a very active rôle in the country's economy.

*The remains of the Mendut Temple are a mile from Borobudur. The roof of the temple gives a good idea of the style and intricacies of the carvings which decorate the temple.*

throughout the islands. Buddhism, a reformed and refined outgrowth of Hinduism based on the teachings of the Indian prince Gotama, was for a time the dominant faith of India. The Indian impact on Indonesia was profound. From the 5th century, a succession of Hindu kingdoms rose and fell until the end of the 13th century, when a mighty Hindu-Indonesian kingdom in East Java grew to become the Majapahit Empire, which united the entire archipelago for the first time.

As political power was concentrated over large portions of the archipelago, the Indonesian people turned more and more towards Brahmanism (traditional Hinduism) or Buddhism. Often a combination of the two was to be found. However, the native religious systems were not completely replaced. They absorbed the new ideas and incorporated them thus producing the highly individual Indonesian-Hindu civilization.

*Worshippers descend the steps of one of the many beautiful and still-used temples which dot the verdant island of Bali.*

## ISLAM

While Arabs came to Indonesia as early as the first century A.D. and Moslems earlier than the 8th century (Islam was founded in Arabia in the early 7th century), Islam did not become established in the islands until the year 1111. By that time, the culture brought across the Indian Ocean by Moslem traders from Persia, western India and Arabia had permeated Sumatra, and its inhabitants were converted to Islam. This was the first foothold of what was to become the predominant religion and way of life on the archipelago.

Islam held great appeal for the people of Indonesia. It seemed well suited to their basic concern for the attitudes towards brotherly love and equality, tolerance and patience, humility and honesty. And as with Hinduism, Islam was assimilated. The Moslem teachers also adopted much that already existed in Indonesian religious practices, as evidenced by the many mosques which retain Indonesian architecture and the many religious ceremonies which carried over earlier concepts.

This willingness to accept new ideas was pointed out by Ambassador Mockarto Notowidigdo in a speech delivered at the 63rd Annual Meeting of the American Academy of Political and Social Science. "Indonesians accept and welcome discussions of problems," said Ambassador Notowidigdo. "And they

*Moslem worshippers gather in front of the Mesdjid Agung, a famous mosque in Djakarta, during Idul Adha (Feast of Sacrifice). Cattle are sacrificed after prayers.*

*Traditional Chinese architecture is represented by this temple.*

*Huge candles burn in the court of a Chinese "klenteng," or place of worship.*

seek compromise. We continually strive for harmony in life and seek to avoid conflict. This does not mean, let us say, that we will not fight for our fundamental beliefs. But to us, conflict is an ultimate and profoundly regrettable last resort, and one to be shunned."

A period of rivalry and conflict between Hindu and Moslem rulers of Indonesia characterized the first 400 years following the introduction of Islam. During the latter part of the 15th century, the first Islamic kingdom arose in Demak and, in 1478, the Empire of Majapahit fell to the Moslems. Its last king chose suicide rather than surrender to the Islamic tide. His son, however, fled with followers to Bali, seeking refuge to preserve and perpetuate their Hindu culture. The isolation offered by the new island home allowed the

*A Moslem girl reads from the Koran. Many contests are held for excellence in interpretive reading from the Koran and competition is keen.*

*The village men perform a welcome dance for famous and important visitors—their costumes an interesting mixture of ancient and modern times.*

growth of a Bali-Hindu civilization that has survived the ages and which flourishes there today.

By the 16th century, Islamic kingdoms ruled all of the archipelago, except Bali.

## MUSIC, DANCE AND DRAMA

Music, dance and drama occupy a surprisingly important position in the cultural life of the Indonesians. Ancient stories and legends, usually based in religion and mythology, are kept alive and vital via the dance and drama accompanied by music.

### DANCE

By and large the dance forms are highly stylized and were originally performed in the courts and temples. Though new dances have been introduced, they retain much of the traditional heritage. The dancers themselves, clothed in elaborate robes and costumes, use gestures which are highly stylized while their faces remain expressionless. Make-up, often very complicated and requiring many hours to

*The classical Srikandi-Tjakil dance depicts the battle between good and evil. Good is represented by the armed maiden, and evil by the masked male dancer. The dancers are pictured in front of the famous Buddhist Temple of Borobudur.*

**41**

*A scene from the Barong dance is performed in front of a temple gate on the island of Bali.*

apply, supplies what "expressions" are required for the performance.

The dances of Java and Bali are probably the most popular. They are certainly the ones most often perfomed. Though similar in many ways—their use of the body positions and postures also can be seen in Hindu sculpture—they vary in tempo and the pace of the movements.

The Javanese dancers were greatly influenced by the Oriental forms and have a more courtly air. The Balinese tend to appear more dramatic and improvisational, and are characterized by sharp stops and broken rhythmic phrases.

### INSTRUMENTS

The music is generally supplied by one of three types of "orchestra." The *gamelan*, most popular generally, is a collection of gongs, string instruments and light percussion instruments, such as metal drums. The tones tend to be high-pitched, with a distinct broken line. The *suling*, or flute bands, enjoy limited popularity. The *angklung* orchestras are made

*Music, an important aspect of Indonesian life, can be heard almost anywhere. Here an orchestra from Bandung plays a traditional concert for the public.*

*The Kechak or Monkey Dance, performed in the village of Bona on Bali, tells the long and involved drama of the legendary monkey army, which figures in the Hindu epic, the "Ramayana."*

*The Legong dance is a highly stylized, early court story-dance. Young girls begin training at the age of 5 in order to perform the many difficult and complicated gestures and steps.*

up entirely of interesting instruments all fashioned from various lengths of bamboo tubes, which are carried or held. This type of music is very popular in West Java.

### PUPPETS

Puppets enjoy an important rôle in Indonesian entertainment. The *wayang golek*, or marionette plays, are seen up and down the archipelago. The puppets have elaborate costumes and are moved about by long, slender sticks. Also popular are shadow puppets. Again, most of the stories or plots have roots in the traditional literature of the islands.

Puppets are such an integral part of Indonesian experience that the government has used them as teaching aids in the educational field.

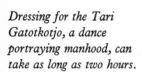

*Dressing for the Tari Gatotkotjo, a dance portraying manhood, can take as long as two hours.*

*Puppet shows hold great fascination for the old and young in Indonesia, attracting crowds at festivals and fairs. The hands and feet of the puppets are operated by long sticks attached to them and moved by the puppeteers. The costumes are often richly embroidered and accurate in every detail.*

### RAMA

Live drama, like the dance, is largely traditional and again uses age-old themes, usually the triumphs of good over evil. Productions can be elaborate with much scenery and many costumes, or quite simple. A *topeng* performance in Bali, for instance, uses only three or four actors, who play all parts among them. But even in traditional semi-religious drama, comedy has a rôle and offers a sharp change of pace to the otherwise serious piece.

## FESTIVALS AND CEREMONIES

The temples and palaces of Indonesia are, perhaps, the greatest single attraction. There are literally thousands of temples scattered across the archipelago. The most famous are the magnificent Borobudur near Jogja, or, as it is officially known, Jogjakarta, which was a Buddhist sanctuary, the Prambanan complex, one of many Hindu-Javanese shrines near

*Gongs such as this are used in a "suling" orchestra.*

*Rituals play an important part in daily Indonesian life, particularly outside of the larger cities. Here a village boy, on the eve of his circumcision, rides a horse through the village accompanied by family, dancers and musicians. The boy is king for a day and receives many presents from family and friends.*

*This boy minds the baby while practicing on one of the percussion instruments used in a "gamelan" orchestra.*

Borobudur; and Bali's largest and most impressive temple, Pura Besakih. The imposing Prambana temples now supply the background for the Ramayana Ballet performances. The performances begin in the early evening, and as night falls, the temples are flood-lit providing the most thrilling and authentic scenery any threatrical performance could possibly have. One says "theatrical" but it is in fact based on the famous Ramayana legend, which is primarily a religious epic concerned with the struggle between good and evil.

Borobudur's design is a mixture of Indian and Indonesian art and culture. It is a solid

*During a public entertainment, President Suharto gives his autograph to a musician dressed in traditional finery.*

*During the Trance Dance, one of the many religious ceremonies in Bali, young girls in a deep trance are carried about on the shoulders of boys.*

monument and not constructed to be entered. It was built around a hill cut to form seven terraces, each representing a level of living on mankind's journey to perfection—the Buddhist conception of the cosmos.

To mention only three of the many temples is an injustice, for no matter where one goes there are interesting and beautiful ones to be seen.

Religious dances, festivals and ceremonies

*Indonesia's popular President, General Suharto, and Mrs. Suharto pay a visit to a village during a local celebration.*

**47**

vivid, gay and serious all mixed together in a grand design whose meaning reaches far back into history.

### CREMATIONS

The great ceremonial cremations of Bali are happy occasions, a time of joy, for it is believed that the soul has finally been set free and can enter heaven. A proper cremation is expensive and requires great preparations. Much money is spent on decorations, ceremonial dances and music, and feasts. The more elaborate the cremation, the greater the prestige. Poorer families bury their dead, but several families will band together to afford a group cremation when sufficient money has been saved.

### HARVEST FESTIVALS

Being the main food of Indonesians, rice is the most important agricultural product. As such, it is understandable that many religious ceremonies are connected with its cultivation and harvest.

are another great tourist attraction. But in general, unless they are specially organized as an entertainment, they are for the Indonesians— those taking part and those observing. There are, of course, pure entertainments, but even most of these are based on historical and religious legends and have many levels of meaning or interpretation.

Bali, "the island of the gods," is famous for its festivals and ceremonies. These range from the very simple to the most elaborate. Almost any excuse, it seems, will do for a celebration in Bali, and the Balinese, a charming and delightful group, spend a great deal of their time in this pursuit.

The birthday of a temple, the *odalon*, calls for a very important and complex celebration. The men decorate the temple building with elaborate bamboo altars, hanging flags and pennants, creating great floral ropes and arrangements. The women prepare vast feasts to which the gods are invited. It is fascinating,

*Harvest festivals are particularly joyful times, with parades to the many temples prior to the feasts and general celebrations.*

*Ferris wheels hold the same thrills and attractions for children the world round and those in Indonesia prove no exception.*

*The new Indonesia— young women compete in the 100-metre race.*

*The Boy Scout movement is popular in Indonesia and the young lads enjoy the activities as do their counterparts in many lands.*

In Java, for instance, the advisor attributes his knowledge and wisdom concerning the ceremonies to Devi Cri, the wife of the god Vishnu. Devi Cri is the patron of agriculture and is also invoked in Sumatra and Sulawesi. Various ceremonies are held at prescribed

*Bull racing is a popular sport in Madura, an important island close to Java. The bulls race in pairs and the driver rides on a ladder-type arrangement which is dragged, having no wheels.*

If there is no horse around, then riding a goat will do, and these boys take full advantage of the opportunity.

The pebble-counting game absorbing these young girls has many names in many countries. In Java it is called "dakon."

The Sukarno Stadium, built in Djakarta for the Asian Games in 1962, seats 125,000 people and is the largest covered stadium in the world.

times, such as before the planting, during the growing period and at harvest time. These ceremonies, often picturesque and always revered, are frequently attended by government officials and local dignitaries.

## ARTS AND CRAFTS

Possibly nowhere in the modern world are so many talented, artistic people collected together as in Indonesia. For centuries the islanders have painted, sculpted, woven and decorated textiles, worked metals and created extraordinary floral pieces. Using their natural sense of art and beauty, they have blended influences from India, Islam, Arabia, and recently the West, with their basic native styles, techniques and themes. The result is a distinct "Indonesian" style that is recognizable anywhere.

Temple carvings of ancient times are less "Indonesian" than contemporary work. The influences were, as with the religions represented by the temples, imported. To the untutored eye the carvings appear to be exactly the same as those to be seen in India, Ceylon, Thailand, Cambodia, etc. The important point,

Cockfighting is still one of the chief spectator sports, particularly in Bali. The birds receive great care and are jealously guarded.

52

*At the 1969 Djakarta Fair, dozens of young women in traditional costume take part in the pagentry.*

*Stone murals such as these, covering great expanses of wall, are popular and require many sculptors and years to complete.*

*Though much new sculpture is created, the forms, patterns and subject matter generally reflect the highly individualistic Indonesian heritage.*

*Wood carving is an esteemed art, especially in Bali, and many works such as this head of a man can be purchased in the shops and villages.*

however, is that the craft and skill remained and were developed. Today's wood and stone carvers are using contemporary life themes which are original and beautiful works of art. The same is true of the country's paintings.

The best wood-carvers in the whole archipelago are to be found on the island of Bali and at Djapara in central Java.

Silver-working is a popular and much-practiced craft. Like the early craft guilds in

*Florid and intricate patterns grow on the gleaming metal, through the skilled craftsmanship of a silver-worker on the island of Java.*

*Metalcraft is an old art in Java, where fine tools, swords and daggers are produced. This man of central Java is making a "kris." The kris, a ceremonial dagger supposedly having magic powers, is used in wedding ceremonies and is a sign of deep friendship.*

Europe, Indonesian artists have tended to collect together in groups or areas. Today the more accomplished silversmiths are located in Jogjakarta, Bali, South Sulawesi and in Sumatra.

The most widely known Indonesian art and craft form is known as batik. Starting with plain cloth, the batik-maker applies a metal die stamp carrying hot liquid wax to areas he does not want to dye, then dips the cloth into a vat. The waxing and dyeing process is repeated once for each kind of dye, until the cloth has an intricate and beautifully delicate pattern.

Batik was originally used for the traditional clothing of both the men and women of Java. In modern times it has gained great popularity and is used extensively throughout the islands and has been adapted to Western styles. Many

patterns are so beautiful that they make impressive wall hangings. The capital of batik-making is Java.

For the tourist, Bali is undoubtedly the mecca of Indonesian arts and crafts for two reasons. The variety offered on the island is great and it is easily accessible. Many of the villages dotting the island practice particular art forms. Most of the Balinese are part-time artists or craftsmen, dancers or musicians.

The Balinese village of Ubud is a painter's paradise, though many artists now live on the beaches of Sanur and Sindu. Batu Bulan produces stone carvers and the village of Tjeluk is famous for its gold and silver craftsmen.

Balinese painting has a long history. Early paintings on cloth were of traditional scenes. In the last three or four decades, modern methods have been introduced and the subject matter is much more contemporary. The visitor has an abundant collection of bright, very lively pictures from which to choose.

*Highly skilled artisans work out designs in the government-owned Batik Research Institute in Jogjakarta.*

*A batik worker paints designs in hot wax on a plain cloth, using a curved pipe-like implement.*

The United Nations Building in New York City has an outstanding example of Balinese painting. The picture, a gift to the United Nations from the Indonesian Government, is the work of Ida Bagus Made.

Weaving, plaiting and embroidery are also popular in the country. Embroidered cloth with its beautiful hues and classic patterns, once used on ceremonial occasions only, is now worn

*An artist works on a mural depicting a scene from the Ramayana legend.*

*Artists begin young in Indonesia, and full concentration is given to the creation of a dancing demon from one of the many folk dramas which play such an important part in the island nation's culture.*

*Exceptionally fine needlework can be found in this bridal gown being created by a Minangkabau lady. Many such pieces of embroidery make attractive wall hangings or may be framed as pictures.*

throughout the islands and is purchased by visitors.

Furniture is another medium in which the Indonesian craftsmen excel. Tables, chests, cabinets, lounges, picture frames, and sofas, all are elaborately carved. Inlay designs use various woods, predominently teak, as well as semi-precious stones, ivory, gold and silver.

Pottery and ceramics have remained largely utilitarian and have not been developed as a major art form.

*Ceramics, an ancient craft, is still practiced in many parts of Indonesia. This potter is from the village of Plered, where pottery-making is the second industry after rice growing.*

Following long-standing custom, these young ladies arrive at the market place with their wares balanced easily on their heads. Great care has been taken to make the food attractive to catch the shopper's eye.

Teeth filing is a must for all Balinese children to qualify them for the after-life, the basic idea being that one should not go to heaven resembling a demon with great fangs. Though it appears nerve-wracking, the process is quite painless.

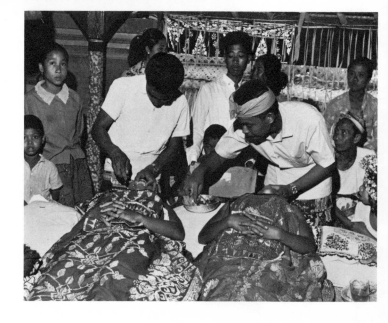

*In the famous terraced rice fields of Bali, at least two crops a year are harvested, and often three or four. The flooded paddies contain young rice plants, and the dry ones hold rice nearing harvest time.*

# 5. THE ECONOMY

*Business as usual at market time—even in the rain—and modern automobiles offer an interesting contrast to the age-old marketing method.*

INDONESIA'S 5-YEAR development plan was begun in 1969. In his message at the end of that year, President General Suharto made the following revealing and encouraging statements:

"All through this year there has been a quieter feeling because the prices of goods, particularly the nine basic necessities, have no longer made jumps. We felt no longer anxious, haunted by the fear of ever increasing prices. Our rupiah has become increasingly stable vis-à-vis foreign currency; not merely for a month of two but all through this year.

"Within three years we were able to put down the inflationary trend from 650 per cent in 1966 to under 10 per cent this year. Last year it was 85 per cent.

"Textile production in 1969 reached approximately 415,000,000 metres, an increase of 30 per cent over 1968.

**59**

*Although this coffee plantation is on Sumatra, the girl picking coffee berries is Javanese. Java was so long identified with high-grade coffee that a slang expression, "a cup of Java," was in common use until quite recently in some English-speaking countries.*

"Industrial production has increased in both quantity and quality. Mining production in such products as oil, tin, nickel, bauxite, gold and silver increased between 5 and 10 per cent over the previous year. Total exports for the year were a little over 1,000,000,000 U.S. dollars. This represents an increase of about 10 per cent."

Evidence of this was presented by the Minister of Foreign Affairs, speaking at a meeting of the American Men's Association. He said: "It is a source of satisfaction to note that by November, 1969, a total of 175 foreign investment projects have been approved amounting to a little more than $1,000,000,000, of which nearly $400,000,000 is of U.S. origin. Besides private foreign investment, the rôle of our foreign trade is even more important and more basic in the promotion of our economic growth."

Indonesia's increasing economic stability and attractiveness to foreign investors is a direct result of the efforts of the present government. Inflation has been all but halted and political calmness reigns. These two factors have made possible a balanced budget, and the implementation of economic and social plans. This new stability in the central government is reflected down to the individual state and local governments, bringing a new sense of security and harmony to the people.

## FOREIGN TRADE

Foreign trade also shows improvement as reflected in the greatly increased foreign exchange earnings. Long existing trade relations with the United States experienced increased activity during 1969. Imports include rice, cotton, wheat flour, machinery, spare parts, aircraft and fertilizers. Exports from Indonesia are crude oil, coffee, rubber and latex products and spices.

## CONSTRUCTION

Notable advances are also being made in the rehabilitation and construction of highways, bridges, irrigation and electrical networks, ports, airports and communications systems.

## PETROLEUM

Indonesia is one of the world's largest producers of tin and rubber, and is the Far East's major producer of petroleum. Petroleum's importance to the Republic is increasingly great, with the growing world-wide acceptance of man-made rubber substitutes, and the resulting decline of natural rubber growing.

New oil fields discovered in 1969 will greatly increase the country's output when they are developed. The largest crude oil storage tanks in Southeast Asia are located at Dumai in Indonesia. However, the principal known reserves are in Sumatra and deep-water terminal facilities have been developed on the island's east coast.

The main oil fields, operated by Caltex Pacific Indonesia (CPI) are located in Minas, Duri, Petani, Bekasap, Pamatang and Pungut. CPI produced 447,000 barrels of crude oil a

*Getting equipment and supplies into oil fields located in dense jungle is a great problem—helicopters have proved the fastest and cheapest method.*

day during 1968. This represents a substantial increase from the 1966 figure of 305,000.

Drilling has proved most difficult as many of the oil fields are located in dense jungle areas. Because road building is a long, tedious and expensive project, helicopters have been widely employed to transport drilling equipment and men to the sites.

Although 50 per cent of CPI is owned by foreign interests, the company is run locally. More than 95 per cent of its employees are Indonesians and over 90 per cent of the supervisory positions are held by Indonesians.

## AGRICULTURE

Indonesia's agricultural potential is as vital a part of the country's economic structure as are its mineral resources. Extensive development projects are high on the priority list of the 5-year plan.

Rich soil, brought down from the mountains by the rivers and streams, has made much of the country rich and fertile. This, coupled with abundant rain and the tropical climate, creates ideal conditions for farming.

Crops which form the chief exports are rubber, sugar, cinchona bark for the manufacture of quinine, tea, coffee, palm oil, cocoa, kapok, tobacco, copra and spices—black and white pepper, cloves, nutmeg and mace.

The main food crops consumed domestically are rice, corn, cassava, coconut, sago, peanuts, soybeans, fruit, sweet potatoes, squash and beans.

The extensive farming projects instituted by the government have assisted in solving two main and most important problems—food production and unemployment. The food production projects, popularly called "Food for Work" have proven quite successful. Other projects also include extensive work on irrigation reservoirs, dams and canals for water distribution. These are essential to increased crop production, particularly rice.

### RICE

Though rice production has increased tremendously, much must still be imported. In 1969, the first year of the 5-year plan, Indonesia achieved its target in rice production. But it is estimated that the country will not be self-sufficient in its rice production until 1973 or 1974. Wheat is not grown in the country and must be imported.

Various international organizations have lent money and technical assistance for developing the projects which are handled by Indonesia's Department of Manpower in cooperation with the Department of Public Works and Energy.

Rice is cultivated on both terraced wet fields (called *sawahs*) or paddies, and on dry fields. Wet fields are by far the most advantageous,

*One of the spices for which Indonesia has long been known is nutmeg, which is the inner seed of a tree which originated in the Moluccas, which are also called the Spice Islands.*

*A Javanese clove merchant in traditional dress displays a sample of his fragrant product. Cloves are the dried unopened flower buds of a small tree of the myrtle family.*

since the farmer has the possibility of reaping more than one harvest per year. In some areas of the country five harvests are obtained in a two-year period—a great boon to both the farmer and the country.

The wet fields, inadvertently, are one of the great sights of Indonesia. It is hard to find anything more beautiful than the great terraced fields of, say, Bali—"giant staircases to the heavens," as they are often referred to locally. To one flying low over their shimmering surfaces, the ponds, reflecting bits of sky surrounded by borders of green, appear as great irregular pieces of smoky mirrors. As the young rice plants begin to grow, the ponds are a brilliant, new green, impossible to imagine.

### OTHER CROPS

Cassava harvests have increased since the building of new tapioca factories and more peanuts are now grown for the manufacture of fine oils and soap.

Coffee, the drink preferred to tea by the Indonesians, is grown in Java, Bali and Sumatra.

Tea is grown in Java and Sumatra as well, and is exported. Java and Sumatra are also the chief tobacco producing areas. The Deli region of North Sumatra grows a tobacco leaf ideal for cigar wrappers and is well known to cigar fanciers.

Java produces most of Indonesia's sugar cane. The sale of sugar is handled by state-owned sugar factories and "sugar syndicates." A syndicate is defined as a group of men who have collected money to buy sugar from the mills. Any businessman may join a syndicate, provided he meets the requirements.

Approximately half of the country's copra is used domestically and the remainder exported. Areas producing the most rubber are on the islands of Java, Sumatra and Kalimantan. Rubber production is also scheduled for increase and the rubber plantations are being modernized and enlarged. Projects also call for the construction of new factories, improving the quality and marketing, and the organization and management of the plantations—both state-owned and privately owned. Of all export products produced on state plantations, rubber ranks first after palm oil.

Although Indonesia's industrial potential is enormous, the country's economy is still largely agricultural. Approximately 80 per cent of the population is involved in some aspect of crop production.

## LIVESTOCK

Though dairying and wool production do not play a big part in Indonesia's economy, cows and sheep are raised for slaughter. Dairying, as it has developed, is a minor industry serving only the larger cities.

Chickens are raised in quantity for both the eggs and meat. While Moslem religious restrictions limit the consumption of pork to non-Moslems, a considerable number of pigs are raised for export.

Work animals are largely oxen and water buffalo. In many parts of the country, the possession of one of these animals is a mark of wealth and prestige.

Horses are bred on the Nusa Tenggara Islands and the famous Sandlewood horse has been developed on the island of Sumba.

## FISHING

The fishing industry, important to the country and economy as a major food source, is large but still incapable of meeting demands.

As with agriculture, the government has initiated plans to increase fishing activities, both in the open ocean off the eastern islands and inland, in the country's many lakes and streams. Foreign technical aid has been accepted and research is underway to improve and develop this vital food source.

Important work in this area is being conducted by the department of oceanography at Pattimura University in Ambon, again with foreign technical aid and experts in the field.

## TOURISM AND TRANSPORTATION

As is true in many parts of the world, tourist traffic to Indonesia is increasing each year. People are curious about this comparatively "new nation" for many and sundry reasons.

Interest runs high over a chain of islands which has supplied the background for a variety of political contests, invasions, and blends of ancient and current cultures.

To most of the people of the world, little is known about this fascinating island republic, though more has been written about it in the last few years than any other comparable area on the planet.

For the experienced traveller, Indonesia offers a new and different experience. For the new traveller, the romance of the "spice islands" and particularly the fabled island of

*Pepper is one of the many spices which traders for generations have coveted and which helped create the legends of the "spice islands." A vine, it is grown on the trunks of trees.*

*Contrasts in old and new are supplied by the traditional Indonesian outrigger canoes and the new, modern Bali Beach Hotel operated by Inter-Continental Hotels.*

Bali, is a great lure. Indonesia's government has wisely recognized the value of this other "natural resource" and is doing much to aid the tourist.

Travel service to and within Indonesia is improving yearly. Garuda Indonesian Airlines, the national carrier of Indonesia, has a fairly broad network outside the country. Internally, it links over 30 cities throughout the islands. Other international airlines have regular scheduled services to the country's two international airports at Djakarta and Denpasar on the island of Bali.

Steamship lines and cruise ships make stops throughout the archipelago and the local steamship company provides inter-island transportation between more than 60 ports.

Surface transport includes bus services, taxi and car hire firms. Most of the major hotels also can arrange bus tours and private cars with guides and drivers. The state railways supply many links to destinations in Sumatra and Java.

New hotels, often under the management of large international chains, have been built, serving the needs and desires of the tourists of many lands. Many smaller, local hotels, often a cluster of guest bungalows around a central building, are available to the foreign visitor. More are being developed.

In all there is much to see and experience in this most unusual country. The government has accomplished a great deal in tourist promotion and current plans are continuing the effort.

## OUTLOOK

The country's economy is truly improving. With new housing and food projects, increased educational facilities, a firmer financial structure resulting from intensive planning and improved management, the 1980's should see a healthy and highly prosperous nation and economy.